The Agony
of
Space and Time

The Agony
of
Space and Time

Shawn McCann

Clere Songbirds
Publishing House

Clare Songbirds Publishing House Poetry Series
ISBN 978-1-957221-17-5

Clare Songbirds Publishing House
The Agony of Space and Time © 2024 Shawn McCann

Printed in the United States of America
FIRST EDITION

Clare Songbirds Publishing House
140 Cottage Street
Auburn, New York 13021
www.claresongbirdspub.com

Contents

Acquiring a Signal

Half of autumn had been stripped away.
The colors still hanging on in the eupohia
of summer's footling dream were vibrate in
the fingertips of the morning sun.
The branches veined the roadway,
shadowing every turn in a psychedelic rush.
The music falling down from the edge of space
was disrupted every now and again
by their flickering over the asphalt dream.
A dream always dedicated to somewhere else
no matter how close to home.
The music eased me out of the bonds
that restrict without mercy.
What was I searching for?
What was I lacking in mind and spirit?
Song after song had me thinking.
My mind a dissonance of mirthless clatter.
Then, by the roadside, a sign,
the words blurring into oblivion,
as words sometime should, caught my eye.
Two children, a boy and a girl not too far apart in age,
siblings would be my guess,
chased each other around the sign.
Their laughter unheard but transmitted somehow
made it known how far I had fallen away.

Stirring

Crossing the street, I could see a young woman
through the windows of a sidewalk café
and my thoughts drifted to another.
The same dark hair, tan skin, a soulful prettiness,
a profile exotic and complete in ancestral detail.
Passing the café on full display
I felt familiar dark eyes taking me in.
Their cruelty shaping an unexpected desire.
I bowed my head to be true to the other woman,
whom could have been her sister,
and whom I have not seen or spoken to in a while.
Time is a dictator, a corrupt arbiter
for the passions lying dormant beneath the skin.
He knows the subtleties and the wants
the passions crave in order to resurface,
the world taking hold—laughing.
His reign restored to the narrow sands of the falling hour.
The blood circulating through the corridors
that comprise me is not mine but his and his alone.
He can rip out of me all passions and claim what's his
anytime he wants, my arms down,
my chest open, I will not utter a word.
No. No. That's too kind. It would be out of character for him.
I'll suffer. I must. I'll feel her in every gesture,
hear her in every fleeting word.
I'll struggle for sleep every night.
The phantom vapor of her perfume encircling me.
My eyes vacant growing dull barely piercing the void
as the hunger for her whisper consumes me.
Can I claim my soul, my need for meekness?
My fight against pride, my struggle to die at the feet of humility?
Can I justify my acetic nakedness with loneliness?
Freewill is hard to contemplate.
Self-abuse will destroy everything I wish to be.
The passion beyond time, mercy beyond mercy,
patient light—more abundant in the darkness of my unworthiness,
please stay with me, my need for you more than I understand.
The remembrance of her eyes, their dark expression never simple,
always searching, her complete and willed insistence on contact.
Her naked shoulder not yet touched by time
leaning into me stirred all that I refused to accept.
Can a restructured hope in this earth-bound struggle for chastity,
the hope both mine and another's mix with the desire for her,
a desire unbound by want, but always subject to time?

The Other Woman

The sun was unkind, sinister even.
Its rays whip-lashes against raw skin.
The day no better, slow like a death knell.
There she was in the sidewalk café,
her prettiness fondly remembered,
coffee in hand, the same hand that gifted me with a seashell
from a foreign land.
A friend was next to her. My eyes only for her.
Her own slow and calm eyes braved the darkness shadowing me.
Drawing closer, the window frame conformed to her,
the same as my dead eyes did when I met her.
I remembered looking away from her that first day.
My eyes downcast avoiding her gaze.
I feared her as all that's shameful fears
humanness deserving of the purest desire.
For I was broken by this world,
enslaved by its own force of will and my lack.
My blanket of kindness filthy, warmed by my meanness.
Contouring my head, my indented pillow of judgments passed.
My lies cradled me in the lullaby of duplicity.
I comforted my unworthiness with the dead of my heart.
Then my shattered gaze climbed to meet hers,
content in the vagaries of human brokenness.
Since I last saw her, I've been dying day by lonesome day.
It's a necessary death, a welcomed death,
a death I don't quite understand.
My executioner's hand impressing on my heart
what I can't pass up,
even though I hurt him day by day, hour by hour,
act by act, word by word.
His nearness my desire.
The dream of my death encircles every thought.
Yet there is no guarantee in my desire for his nearness.
My death still incomplete. My guilt a gratuity self-applied,
a paralyzing proof of dryness, a sticky patchiness unquenched.
The stony path to my prison cell an inescapable memory.
Her tan skin, her long dark hair,
her slender and humble frame were close by.
I could feel her. My blood ached in the recognition.
The sharp stab of mortality unmasking my pain.
The knowledge of someone special grows more agonizing
in the need for chastity.

She sensed my anger.
Her soulful dark eyes dropped from my dead eyes.
I wished I could have told her how this world is winning the war.
The war I chose to wage in a salvo of despair and disillusionment.
Then maybe she would have been able to feel
my hapless will trying to shed my skin,
my struggle to reclaim my soul. Maybe she could have envisioned
my head bowed at his feet? His hands spread over me?
His blood matting my knotted hair—
one drop of his commingling with mine is all I need,
as he blows the embers of my name
into the vast nothingness of un-memory.
Then and only then could I look at her with truth, with honor.
I stood on the corner waiting for the light to change.
My head bowed
as my mind's eye embraced the poetic longing for her curves.
Why was I scared? I should have turned back just to say,
"Hi. I haven't forgotten you. I still care. Your kindness, I miss."
My ugliness was too strong. I traced its geography on my face.
My fault too deep, too brutal. I felt its rupture splitting my heart.
I could not bring myself to gaze upon the very meaning of her name.

Beyond the Wake

His arms, a little boy's, lay flat
on the weathered railing at the end of a dock.
His right hand atop his left.
His head crowned them in youthful glory.
His face was bent toward the river's murmur.
His forehead reddened by a day's worth of sun.
His ginger hair lightly kissed by the same dying sun.
My guess was that the river's mirror
distorted the freckles I couldn't see.
He did not give the tour boat we were on the slightest glance,
and I wondered what unworldly treasures
flowing through his mind separated us from him.
Then I glanced around the boat
watching the men and women
making eyes with each other.
Their stares empty with want.
I listened to their talk about titles and educations,
worthy awards and unmatched accolades,
and the money that follows,
always dragging useless commodities along.
I set my beer down, lowered my eyes,
and weaved through the crowd to the stern.
I watched the figure of the boy against
the red rim remnants of the already forgotten sun,
recalling all that I have lost in my own shaping of want.
When the boy was completely lost to the darkness,
the palaver of the boat polluting the slow night,
suns not ours lighting into existence,
I lowered my gaze and knew the wake I could not see beyond
was unequal to the flowing mirror returning his.

Beyond this World is Kindness

Her womanhood was sacrosanct.
She wrapped her arms tightly around
her upturned knees, immovable against
the prying eyes of brokenness.
Their ruthless cravings for her
chopped down any good
that still may have danced from them
in the bygone gestures of childlike wholeness.
She lowered her gaze from their glowers
of hostility and unmitigated demand.
She escaped to the breath of childhood,
the warmth still there in the
dream of fugitive recognition.
Her thoughts returning to the
only boy she ever loved.
They killed him a long time ago with words.
His death unmercifully drawn out.
The wounds of which were filled in
by the poison of their signifiers.
She has been searching for another like him,
but their eyes, so many eyes, were unlike his.
In this vast hopelessness, she decided to live beyond
this world's web of unmanliness and misogyny.

If I Could Paint

She moved through the crowd
detached from the commonplace ethos of ambition
and the banal impetus of wealth.
Her eyes silent to the eyes
trying to swim through her.
Both men and women awash with eagerness
hoping for that solitary bridge
lifting them to recognition.
They could not fathom the current of her depth.
I watched her from the heart aching distance
that is the safety of my own inter-passivity;
for knowing her would have been
like a rock disturbing the calmness,
the murkiness stirred-up
a by-product of my own meager ambition.
Her long dark hair parted in the middle,
flowing down past her shoulders,
covered her profile in perfect aloneness.
I refused the subtle shape of her breasts
and the slow measure of her curvy stride.
If I could paint, my eyes roaming freely
among the colors. My brush honest
matching her aloneness, and my mind earnest
in depth, I would paint her with
the imperfection she desires.

Indian Summer

Below us the stream's chortle flowed slow and melodious,
aloof to everything other than time.
Dying harmony in the trees rising above us,
the leaves' orchestra shimmering in
the requiem of the ebbing sun.
The river bank ours, if only for a moment,
molding our imprint,
its earthiness a memory
of our bodies sharing the same space,
the same hope, the same fear, the same note.
My body a pocket for yours
as the slight chill of a new season
intermingled with the dwindling warmth of another.
The two drawn together like leaden lovers
tragically unaware their brief song is dying.
You lifted your hands from my knees
sliding them over mine,
interlocking our fingers effortlessly.
Your touch, your gift, an exigent charge.
The fit was an artist's creation—
our conjoined instruments of discovery.
Your sensuality guided me to your lap, my last respite.
You waited and waited.
I felt your body slipping down into mine
wanting me to swallow you in the hunger only lovers feel.
Your dark hair teased my chin.
Your body, rising and falling
in the cadence of your slow and thoughtful measure,
tried to coalesce with the un-embraceable.
Your hands squeezed mine lightly.
You turned your head.
I slowly leaned mine back.
My eyes traced your profile.
You felt them holding you.
Your own gaze holding space,
wide-eyed and sincere.
I moved to speak.
Your eyes shifted.
The wind blew.
An unexpected chill cut through us.
Your gaze slipped to an eddy of dead leaves,
a sadness that has forever shaped me.
You stood and blew me a kiss.

Our silent song separated.
Your eyes were moist.
A tear escaped, then another, then you.
The silence regained, greedy and savage,
in an instant mine alone again.
In the gaps between your naked movements
you could not place my inertia,
and I could feel the eurhythmy
that you alone had begun to establish
fading away bit by lonely bit.
Ineffectuality is a brittle cloak draping the dead.
I wish I could have shown you
how I ached for the rhythm
of your warm breath,
or how I longed to live in the gift
of your body's supple release.
I am a virgin again cloistered in loss.

Broken Dream

In the darkness
before dawn
I had to go
someplace
and deliver news
I didn't want to.
The next moment
I was reclining on my couch.
A woman appeared from the hallway.
Her dark hair sleep-shaped.
Her prettiness framed by the morning's odd freshness.
She was in her pajamas and slippers,
a robe wrapped tightly around her.
I opened my arms and said to her,
"You are only my sister,
 but I need someone close right now."
A sister which in reality I don't have.
She replied, "I've been waiting for this moment a long time,"
and snuggled in close to me
laying her head on my shoulder.
I could feel two heartbeats sharing the same blood.
Then out of nowhere,
sitting on her lap,
appeared a bi-racial little girl
smiling peacefully at the scene.
No other words were spoken.
Then I awakened.
The dawn lifted.
My blinds dingy in the gray light.
A wave of sadness swept over me.
My mind miserable.
My eyes dead.
I knew the day would be long and lonely.
To interpret the dream would be to fail it.

The Un-dreaming

i don't even dream of women any longer
those fantasies of conjoined hands
interlaced fingers
entwined bodies
communal limbs
the vineyard of two simple souls growing together
all of it pulverized into an unknown chaos
floating helplessly away from the pull of gravity
slipping by the dying lamps of hope
i settle in for a contemplative life
lacking impetus
threadbare and fatigued
lonely
action and speech lacking fire
lacking compassion
lacking value
lacking virtue
impotent
Anger triumphant in my portrait of commission
fear and self-loathing in my mirror of omission
i played cruelty's game and lost
i'm playing now
losing
desire devolving into want
want turning into Lust
selfishness... the worst?—tell me
—they all feel the same
enemies of the Spirit breathing Death
equality among Death's followers?
Pride brutal Pride
stronger than all
thought after thought
steam rolling on
barreling past
the Humility of Another's heartbeat
the Passion of Another's hand
Another's voice
Another's feel
Another's suffering
love... Another's Love.

Palm Sunday

Y2K had been reduced to a sly smile from history.
Actually, the new age fear entirely forgotten by now.
The years assumed their regular speed
and I was now looking in on thirty,
single, fatherless, sexless, but feeling no pressure from a world
where certain All-American standards must be obtained
before the side long glances are cast and assumptions are made.
It was a late winter Sunday with no hint of spring in the air.
Hamlet was being performed at the Syracuse Stage
and I could not wait for the opening act.
I wanted the broodiness
and the conscious riddled ghost
of the tortured Hamlet to speak to me,
like his father's ghost had spoken to him
setting him on a path to death,
for vengeance is synonymous with death.
Hamlet remained silent.
The kinship of ruminations
and crafty soliloquies were exaggerated by me only:
a want-to-be Hamlet devoid of convictions
and fearful of eternity's slumber.
It was Ophelia who drew my eye,
pinched the flesh of my ear lobes.
She was an African-American actress
doomed by her aloof Hamlet,
who, standing over her grave,
ostentatiously exhaled his love for her.
At one point, emotively,
Ophelia dropped to her hands and knees,
her bodice holding her breasts perfectly,
and I felt the pure emotion of her performance—it was ecstasy.
My friend during the intermission commented on her cleavage.
I felt out-of-place that I couldn't share in his excitement.
Her performance was a desire beating beneath the flesh,
and her flesh a mere blanket of that desire.
After the performance while driving home I was
thinking of this princess that would never be
and how the prince failed her.
I pulled into a Wendy's for a quick dinner;
a dinner one could brood over in this day of unending Hamlets
with their unending desires to be seen and heard and felt.
The pretty young woman at the drive thru window

looked into the back seat of my car
and noticed my palms from Mass
laying over the books
that offered me everything this world could not.
She simply said, "I forgot it was Palm Sunday," and sighed.
As she passed me my food, I passed her a palm.
She smiled and thanked me holding the palm softly in her hand,
and I knew Ophelia, wherever she was, smiled too.

Two Women

The darkness lurched over the water.
Its ripples drowsy and dreadful.
The darkness, seen from a quaint hilltop,
unusually deliberate, coming in on an edge of madness,
settles in making its simple overtures,
its agonizing passes,
with wrinkled hand to wrinkled hand,
belabored heart to belabored heart,
and unfulfilled dream to unfulfilled dream.
I stared wide-eyed into the impenetrable blackness,
and glimpsed the soft sadness of being.
I am pulled by the gravity of two women,
imperfection upon imperfection of myself,
the highlight in their guarded gazes,
with their eyes set aglow amid the transient dark,
now bemused by my new fighting presence.
Still, later, every imperfection was tethered
to the melody of the morning,
where the hypnotic pink hue
suffused by the beckoning blue,
was left alone to meet the awakening dawn.
The new sky was layered and poetic,
and yet it did not ease the dramatic pull of the two
women whose faces I could no longer remember.

Veiled Desire

There she was
standing before her office door.
Her flaxen hair
and soft countenance
veiled by her coat,
the color of which is lost to memory.
In the fog of my mind's fragility,
I think I can say
the color was neutral;
a compliment to the slow
claim of the new season.
She stood straight.
Her door closed
as she rested her hand
on the door knob.
The last time I was near her,
she held a frigid posture,
only showing me her back.
Her face concealed.
My heart ached
as her father tested my senses
A tease? A gesture? Both?
In this new seasonal playground
of misinterpreting dreams,
with their separation
and strange coherence toward reality;
a season, which is nothing
more than a common fall,
she drew up my gaze to contemplate
the template of my growing desire.

Winter's Waning

The tiresome asphalt,
arteries of modernity's
just and unjust movements
of commerce, of rubber, of war,
cut through the dark shades
of time's compression.
Weight upon weight
allowing each other
its chosen voice.
Dipping beneath time's tongues
of fire, of disaster, of completion and renewal,
with our digital obsession
losing its voice, its own tongue searching
for a forked and uncompromising mark.
Moving on, my wheels churning with desire,
my own bifurcated tongue, dry with un-want,
accompanied by dull eyes is unsatisfied.
The gaze of which I scan the hills of white
before sinking into the defiles
of upright naked brown,
of mud, of midden, of rotten choices.
The turkey vultures take up
the space of barrenness, of sequestered lust.
Across in a twin plot of land,
the geese and crows share space.
In between this asphalt nightmare,
this Goyaesque depiction of the valley and of the sky,
the blackbirds, the swallows, the American Robins
and the occasional red flash of a cardinal,
dart to the safety of the slumbering branches.
Above the hawks and an eagle
glide and swoop with eyes of fire.
Eyes and movements I can only
recall in the serenity of a heavenly dream.

Last Thoughts Before Sleep

At night, in bed, I am just a man alone thinking about
how one-year skips casually by into the next.
This thought is wedged in between
the last worthless words on the television
and the recounting of my own from the day
as I am forever compelled to do,
always leaning one way or the other in their rightness
or wrongness.
The sheets still cold I turn and face the bedside lamp
hoping to shed the darkness of another day
devoid of another's body to touch;
a body simmering with one-half of a synergy
in need of a match;
her energy wordless and saying everything.
For now, I just lay back and ponder an empty hand
wishing for the caressing of fingers
along the downy hairs of arms and legs and stomachs.
Each body laughing gently into the shadows
that hold everything
without gesture or retelling.
Of course, this night will have its Freudian approach,
jostling me between the unconscious
and the sub-conscious minds,
the battle raging-on like two lonely combatants
refusing to lay down their arms just to let each other live.
I'll dismiss whatever the night brings,
longing for that one special body to touch,
not with repression or misplace desire,
or a mother lost somewhere in the id of libidinal longings.
The night will pulse with the compassion
and the simple human necessity—
or maybe it's just my human necessity—
to have a heart pumping next to my own,
imperfection matching imperfection,
and never worrying about its opposite
no one living on this dichotomy of dirt can claim anyway.
Just before the dimming of the light,
my eyes turning inward,
my skull a tabernacle of everything human,
I hope to dream of a steady breath not in complacency
or in the rush of settlement but in the steadiness of another's flame
that one night may burn slowly and peacefully beside my own.

A Roman Smile

My passport unburdened by stamps
was safely concealed in my neck wallet.
Thinking about a warning to tourists
I would reach-up from time to time just to make sure it was there.
The irony of the David and the bench
wrapped around his backside a day and a train ride away.
The steps of St. Peter's Cathedral
and the crowd behind gazing up at
sun drenched altar of the Palm Sunday Mass,
only two days old, seemed as distant as my first communion.
My mind was stuck on the Pieta, my favorite sculpture.
The camera was steady in my hands, my mind was clear,
focus wasn't a concern. Still, the blurring of the unblemished
youthfulness and sadness of the Madonna
looking down on the serenity of her Son's face unsettled me.
I was beyond the walls of Vatican City
somewhere on the outskirts of Rome,
knowing I would not be going back.
If I were a soothsayer and could clearly see the sunset
over the Eternal City on Good Friday night,
or the young lovers that same night
gathered around the Trevi Fountain
asking me to take their pictures,
each framed smile bright and clear,
I think I would have eased back on the judgment of myself.
Those were days away, and my mind and the moment were one.
I can't even remember the piazza I stumbled into
or the bar I stopped at sitting outside at a table
scrolling through the twenty-seven pictures,
each picture more disconcerting than the last
of the Mother and Child
who have set me on the journey to the agape.
The beer in front of me was getting warm as I blamed my hand,
the corruption brought from home, the ugliness of my heart,
the beam in my eye, every stain seen and unseen,
imagined and unimagined.
I leaned back in my chair and looked across the piazza.
She was looking at me. Her eyes were set and unwavering.
She was tall, dark and pretty—a Roman no doubt.
Her eloquent and undeterred stride
of looking at nothing new told me that much.
Feeling my ugliness of the moment I quickly bowed my head.

I set my camera to the side and slowly twirled my glass of beer.
I did not want to look up, yet I had to she was that pretty.
When I did, she was a few feet away, her eyes resting softly on me.
She smiled and I returned the smile happy that we spoke.

A Simple Gesture

When she asked me which I preferred,
a pebble or seashell form Ghana,
her dark eyes shining,
I said seashell without any afterthought.
She handed me the shell and walked away.
Her long dark hair falling over the small of her back,
an exotic creature in her own right.
For safe keeping I placed the shell in my breast pocket.
At home, alone with my thoughts,
I turned the shell over in my hand and wondered.
The shell, no bigger than my thumb nail, seemed insignificant;
the bowl of its underside no more than a tear catcher perhaps;
two tears would breach its rim,
three tears would drown it in an ocean of sorrow.
Then I thought about hope and wondered what it meant.
Was it in the next naked body other than my own?
Hers perhaps with her tan skin and slender frame
a better offering than I can give,
or was it something beyond the ephemeral;
something bright and true,
a voice echoing through the darkness of my mind,
freeing me from the years of exile and solitary confinement.
Or was it in the simple and intimate gesture of a friend
that began on the Ghana shoreline,
traversed an ocean overflowing with shells,
and then began again when the shell was passed
from her hand to mine,
her smile stronger than words.
I prefer to believe hope is in the gesture,
something sincere and undying.

Broken Wing

Mid-morning, in between appointments for work,
I snuck home for the usual reason
if anyone bothered to ask,
holding me accountable for my whereabouts
with a sly question or two.
I've made this detour, the proverbial a million times,
with nothing other than relief on my mind.
When I pulled into the driveway
he was standing there alone in the sun
at the edge of the dried-up lake bed of an old oil leak.
He looked on seemingly unmoved by my front-end
towering toward him like the Death Star.
He was an American Robin,
common to New York;
first confirmed by an ex-friend's
handbook to northeastern birds
and then reconfirmed via the internet.
As I approached him cautiously, he defecated,
perhaps out of fear or need or both;
that is when I noticed his wing
caved in and immovable.
When I leaned over for a better look,
my head eclipsing the sun,
he tried hopping away from the shadowed
totality of my head on legs resembling
the discarded stems of spent marijuana buds.
I coaxed him into the shade of the garage
thinking a bed of plush grass was a better place to die.
The thought that maybe the sun was warm against
the cold coursing through his body never occurred to me.
What really bothered me were the flies
ruffling up his feathers that were no longer needed,
and how each one of them seemed to be taking turns
climbing over the white ringed orbs of his dark eyes.

Disjointed Thoughts

Life has become mundane.
My being is in a daze.
My heart is lost struggling alone somewhere
In the terrain of unspoken truths,
craving the thoughts
        and the feelings that mean something, anything.

I drive from street to street,
        the city changed and unchanged,
my hometown of dread and despair,
        a portrait I can't lift a hand to help mend.
I lack gumption and strength.

Humility is just a mirage,
        and sacrifice is a punctured thought bubble
leaking away into an obscurity of a tortured dream.
I want the heat and the war of words to stab me in the heart
repeatedly
        provoking fight and desire.

I need the children's eyes, green, blue, brown, gray,
        any color of those glassy souls
to stir the remnants of a past scarcely recognizable.

The woman walking past me, her steps slow and soft,
to draw-up my head
        from my concrete loneliness,
my steps heavy transforming into the lightness of hope,
        matching her steps when our eyes meet.

That was today. Tomorrow will be the same.
        Life will go on,
my shadow shrinking from its offering.

Beside My Bed

Edward Hopper's *Summer Interior*
has always stuck with me,
like the sunset disappearing behind a drive-in movie screen
just before my first kiss.
The movie unremembered, the girl forgotten
and then remembered when time demands it.
Early on I realized life moves on like a TV screen,
keeping me idle and numb, or should I say dumb,
filling me with a desire of all that I am not
and all I'll never need or even want
once the silence reclaims the night
and all that I am and should be.
The stroke of the brush is different.
The palette tilted in the artist's hand.
His eyes moving from the canvas to the colors,
his brush creating mixtures I'll never understand.
That's the vision that keeps me up at night
stirring emotions and desires that refuse to die.
Every time I look at Hopper's *Summer Interior*,
the woman as close as she wants draws me in
by her presumed sliding off of the bed tense with loss
or maybe just heavy with the plain absence of another.
Her down turned face is hidden from view,
with her dark hair the perfect contrast to
the simple white tank top covering her breasts—a delicate touch.
Her left arm is straight. Her body supported by the disheveled bed.
Her left hand is buried beneath the milky expanse of her thighs,
with her legs angled at her knees running parallel to the bed.
Her dark pubic hair wide at the top and tapering down behind
the protection of where her forearm narrows into her wrist.
Every time I look at her the aloneness of my room fades into hers.
My eyes disturbing the privacy of her window
establishes my voyeurism only for a moment
before her half-naked aloneness reshapes mine into loneliness.
I won't give her a name for fear of losing her.

The Shadow Before the Door

Every compliment brings
to the surface
of my being
my shadow self.
Then the compliment
slips back to the
voice that uttered it.
The compliment is nothing more
than a full moon glimpsed
at the corner of a window pane
just before a restless sleep.
The only thing that remains
is the ugliness of my nightmares.
The subterranean wound opens
swallowing the faded scar
of some unknown or forgotten sin,
only to scab over and spread
into a larger more distinct,
more painful scar.
The scar's sister shape
carves out a corridor in my brain,
its depth of darkness
binds me fearful waiting for judgment.
My carapace of immorality
waiting to be ground to dust,
as my being lonely and tattered
waits before a door that,
like for Josef K., is meant for me only.

Time's Kingdom

Her voice, the breeze of freshness, of hope,
teased the trees where we chased each other in laughter.
The game was always best in the rain.
The canopy provided some coverage.
The smell of the wet earth held ceremoniously
then released with each breath.
The green of the leaf cleaner, more vibrant.
The rain eased us in and out of silence.
In the momentary silences, in between the laughter and name calling,
we narrowed our gazes scanning the population of tree trunks,
with the promise of the season speaking all around us.
Even the weeds fed from the rain's promise
and grew unafraid from the downward swoop of the scythe.
When we heard the sound of our footsteps begin again,
we left them uncounted never worrying
about where they may lead us.
We were just trying to match the unknown
where of our bodies through the brown and green
of a forest we once used as our own palace.
We were the king and queen in the ceremony of young love;
not the love of two bodies becoming one
and then when done simply undone.
We were just two kids lost in the possibilities
of all the wild dreams that eventually escape with the wind,
doing our best to hide the tense and dreaded anticipation
of the alarm clock of our parents' voices calling us home for dinner.
Years later I used to think of her now and again
and wonder if she remembers the forest;
to remember me never entered my mind,
the thought too mundane, the need inconsequential.
One day I decided to drive by the forest
and found nothing but a small tract of wooded land,
and undisturbed brambles swallowing former trails.
The thought to walk through the trees one more time
quickly fell away like the lonely descent of the last leaf.
The wood itself was doing nothing but separating the old cemetery
from the neighborhood we once lived and believed in.
Like decaying bones unable to support their own weight
half the trees were dead and falling over each other.
The other half beginning to slump into tinder waiting for their time.
As I swept her from memory,
I drove away, and my eyes slipped
from the rearview mirror down to the road ahead.

Morning

The blood moon rose over the Atlantic.
The tide was high as the moon's light slanted inland
and out over the uncompromising sea.
Leaning over a balcony railing I followed the light
down the shrinking sands of the littoral zone
and thought about the symmetry of the moon,
the ocean and the bight of the shoreline.
I was alone and my heart beat:
Perfection… Perfection… Perfection.
A subdued eureka moment in a life
borne into the imperfections of longing,
the dissymmetry between body and soul, and the mind's attack.

I eased back from the railing,
my Jameson-on-the-Rocks half empty, and sat down.
I smiled thinking about all the brave men and women
toiling over the sea.
In a moment of loneliness—
an ephemeral moment of kinship with mother earth,
I thought that to die in the cold darkness of the water,
with the full moon shining down,
was the final perfection
for all those holding onto a kiss unlocked by land.
Then I thought what if I was one of the brave and the ocean my home.
I dreamed about my last breath,
the rapid drumming of my heart ceasing.
My eyes falling silent in the sublittoral darkness,
entombed within the salinity of her power.
Then hopefully all that's good and right
birthing me back into a world
divested of anger and pride and hatred,
a world of gentleness and light.

I awoke in the morning,
my arm hanging toward the ground, my hand empty,
and I looked down at the tiny shards
of glass twinkling in the sunlight.
The balcony floor was dry and I rubbed my eyes
looking between the spindles of the railing.
The tide was out, its tumble and roar as gentle as a lion cub's.

The embrace of the sun found a few bodies to warm.
I walked inside leaving the shattered glass and ocean behind.
The bathroom mirror held the redness of my eyes:
eyes that have seen and that have lied.
I walked to my bedroom and closed the door
leaving the tumble and roar at the threshold,
and fell into a familiar darkness and slept a dreamless sleep.

Rainy Night Refrain

The light from the street lamp,
blurred and defiant of the dark,
fingered the gaps of our tattered blinds.
The rain drumming against the roof
infusing its rapid thudding against the hard ground
grips the silence of the room,
embracing everything the silence claims as its own.
Their ensemble spreads out a certain command over our bodies.
It's a song nobody can claim as theirs's.
The song belongs to the earth,
its fertile rhythm a blessing,
and we listen without speaking,
hoping the will to hear begins before thinking.
You breathe-in deeply and release.
Your breasts rise and fall against my body with ease.
Skin against skin, the friction undoing
the desquamations of loneliness,
but the warmth between us is unequal,
and I am saddened for I feel I fail you.
Although you understand my aversion to trust,
you push forward anyway and begin to speak softly,
an unarmed attempt to draw me closer.
I listen naked as each syllable that falls from your lips
joins the chorus you believe you will me to hear.
The silence, the rain, and you,
a portrait I struggle to feel, to hear, to believe.
Deafness seizes me and the sleep of the undeserving overtakes me.
Still, the next rainy night I'll struggle for you in the gathering dark,
my meager caress, all I can offer,
bridging the deep chasm of thought,
should die happily upon the nakedness of your sincerity.

The Dominatrix and the Intellectual

She was a waitress at the bar I used to hang at.
She was new and pretty with dark hair and dark eyes.
Her body a seductive museum of ink.
On the side she was a dominatrix,
or so I heard through the scuttlebutt circling the joint;
but every time she looked at me her eyes were soft,
far from the leather, the whip and the demand of chains.
When business was slow, she would settle on me
speaking simply of the everyday.
Her voice advancing and retreating with delicacy.
Maybe it was a ploy by a seasoned dominatrix,
a strategy to disarm and then humiliate,
if I were so inclined to accept the role.
Deep down I don't think it was.
There was compassion in her voice.
Her eyes an unspoken understanding beyond the everyday.
On some days her boyfriend would come in
and sit at the bar nursing a beer I never heard of.
He could have been one of Ginsberg's "angelheaded hipsters"
howling into the madness and horrors of the night.
One day I noticed through the tone of his body language
he shunned us denizens at the bar
as you would the middle finger of a buffoon.
I suppose our talk was too vapid for his consideration,
and he seemed to know,
by way of the epistemological nature of his thought,
that the Enlightenment to us was nothing more
than an extended happy hour.
I watched him once, his eyes seeming to stray subconsciously,
although at a closer look, more deliberate than anything else,
from the pages of Nietzsche's On the Genealogy of Morality.
The book was propped-up on the bar and flared open,
his marginalia ubiquitous and bold,
and, if I had to guess, magnanimous.
I chalked-up his awareness to something hypersensitive,
something nurtured from years of intense thought,
something very few of us possess.
In between his readings I'm sure he pondered Jean-Paul Sartre
and Camus and the depths of existentialism,
and, needless to say, by way of deductive reasoning,
he understood Dostoyevsky
better than Dostoyevsky himself ever did.

I often wondered what his philosophy of life may have been,
and what I may have missed not befriending a cat like him.
Still, what I thought about most during my friend's employment,
and am stuck wondering about it to this day,
is the tattooed tear protecting her story.

The Shaping of the Unseen

She ran her hands softly over her stomach.
Her brown eyes were wide and elsewhere
gazing through her hands circling
over the unseen form growing within.
"He's been quiet all day," she said and looked up,
her hands still caressing the unseen.
I could see the thought of an unsure future gaining ground in her eyes,
and I waited patiently interested in a story other than my own.
Her story, equipped with the catalysts, the plot turns,
and the subconscious subtleties of human nature,
would drive any pursuer of the human drama
right into the immensities of her heart.
The pendulum of which was swinging between
the darkest of its depth to the lightest of its light.
Aristotle would have been proud of her story;
a story just as old and fresh as the flesh and blood of former tales
heard from generation to generation.
All the players, with different names and different faces,
nothing more than abstract forms from foreign places,
would parallel her narrative from the beginning,
the middle and the end.
Her tripod capturing another portrait of the human condition.
Even though her tale would have held the Ancients silent,
each one with chin in hand waiting for the next line,
it was still her story to tell not mine,
a lowly poet sitting next to her
thinking of all the eras before my own,
now sadly aware of slipping through the postmodern grip
only to land helplessly into the apathetic clutch of the digital age.
Still, a poet, searching for a voice to lend me my own
before falling silent again.
Thus, when she handed me her phone
showing me the 3D sonogram of her child,
I thought about the Renaissance,
and how the image of her unborn child
resembled an unreleased form
from a disfigured piece of marble.
Then my thoughts quickly turned
to Michelangelo's struggle with the unseen,
his brow furrowed, his eyes intent, his instinct unwavering,
his hammer and chisel working out of stone the marble of creation.

Silent Apology

The lake stills at dusk
holding the pink and striated reflections
of the last claim of day.
The night creatures take the air
no longer encumbered by the
waning virtues of a long summer's day,
shortening already leaning toward fall.
The lake fed by the surrounding peaks
of a winter long forgotten accept the burden
of our waste and humanity.
The children play on from morning
to evening and well into the night.
How delightful it is to remember
nothing but the small misfortunes
that a parent could remedy with
a slight pass of a hand removing
the vagrant strands of hair from their
fresh and furrowed brows,
and their eyes set on nothing
but the small promises of tomorrow.
Now I lean back and gather in the next generation,
watching every child, and apologize
to them all in the small silences of my mind,
knowing that their burden will
be much heavier than mine.

To the Coming Promise

The dark rim of the mountains serrates the alpenglow.
The children gather in around the promise of firelight.
Their faces set aglow in untouched youthfulness.
Their laughter skipping across the mirror of water
sun-drenched and unobservant of time,
and I sit alone thinking about you,
circumventing the scales of loneliness and thought,
writing poetry to the first whisper of night.
What is lost will forever be lost.
What is gained nobody can say.
I'll move on looking for the few scraps of truth yet unfound,
carrying no resentment of what is left behind.
The seasons move fast now, time set in hyper drive,
accelerating up to the unknown platitudes
the aging can always cling to finding the will to move on.
From the windows of my soul,
the world blurs into barely decipherable shapes
allowing my imagination to remake
reality into a montage of life and death
and everything left over.
I know I must accept the sorrows of time,
each vagrant memory peeling away
to drift alone in the wind and disappear.
For death is personal and intimate,
a solo act even in the midst of many.

Simplicity

This country we claim as ours
boiling over from the fissures of hate and race.
This world we claim we love we trample and chop down.
The meekness of the forgotten slowly suffocating,
thirsting for peace.
The resources from a past destruction
drying-up from finite wells.
Nature's holiness stripped naked by the smiling virtues
contained in distorted mirrors.
The extreme reach of each religious sect
claiming their sole right to be loved by God,
whereas God's love extends over all,
unbound by the creeds of the faithful and the unfaithful alike.
Simplicity. Simplicity. Where are you?
Beyond your clear shores all is turbid,
and I am mired in things we claim to understand,
but misinterpret with venom.
So, I turn my hope to the midnight flower
spreading for the moon alone, silent and un-shattered.
Her petals extending softly upward.
Her fragrance wafting toward the guardian of night
and then closing at the first caress of the sun,
understanding that refection
is sometimes better than direct touch.
I welcome the infant's soft cry rising above
the borrowed heads of a silent church.
Her sermon intermingling with the priest's sermon.
The priest's voice breaking with humility
stumbles toward an unknown destination.
Their songs the bookends of mortality,
their hearts allied in gentleness.
The blue jay on a bough of the cherry tree
that refused to blossom for me.
The turning of his head like a mechanical clock,
and I focus in on him hoping for recognition,
while wishing for the hollow bones of flight
from a tree that is no longer mine.
The light in the window from a parent,
his body understanding death and its demand
would not allow him to stay up.
The light a beacon for a son balding,
descending into his mid-fifties,

a grandson, no longer a child but childless, moved profoundly,
understanding for the first time a parent is always a parent
and a child always a child.
For the exotic young woman in a red dress.
Her curves the very essence and warmth of summer.
Her eyes sighing without a sincere goodbye.
Her body shaping the subtle but strong fibers
stitch by stitch beneath the lights
that will soon blur into discontent.
The blood pumping through her veins fueling a heart that
knows the simplicity of a seashell.
Simplicity. Simplicity. Simplicity.
The word caught in the narrow confines of my throat.
That's all I can hope for before my heart turns cold
from the things I cannot control.

The City of My Soul

My soul is a dilapidated city.
     The winds of perpetual darkness
hollow through unguarded vacancies.
     The passage to the other side raging.

Hesitant to ford the river's anger,
     its fury one-sided,
I pace the river's edge,
     my head down, my hands buried in my pockets,
my eyes contemplating this border of despair.

I set my gaze on the particles
     of light orbiting in the ecstatic chaos of the other side,
a place where the darkness
     is dethroned forever.

My toes teased the water's edge.

I threw my rope at your feet.
     I set my last and unspooling hope on your pity,
but I drowned.

My last vision your eyes.

My last sound your laughter.

My last love—you.

I floated down to the coldness
     of my last depth.

The Dead Above

The leaves with no longer anything to claim,
windswept, wayward, brittle, blanket the graves.
The deciduous still incomplete dully painting the countryside
holds onto the last of spring's flowering.
The dirt below growing colder inch by inch
waits for the coming winter.
The brittle bones' beneath,
matching the shifting blankets above,
could not care less that the etched-out names,
no longer theirs but the stones, are covered;
or that they warm-up later in the afternoon.
The sun's gesture still there in the growing distance
understands life for the dead has been released
from this churned-up earth,
the sometimes blankness of earthly thought,
the disorder of being, and the pain.
The inhabitants above the dirt turn to the beliefs
that occupy a small corner of thought.
Walled-in by a perfect silence
their loved-one's unknown whereabouts
are given consideration during a brief moment of time,
or at church when the dead are prayed for,
or in the middle of a grocery store line,
eyes wide as the conveyor belt moves their daily essentials along,
or at a party where the dead's name is mentioned here or there.
Their hope clings to an idea.
Their hopelessness clings to an alternative.
Still, the voice of nothingness will have its say:
the last and thinnest reflection,
a thought even the most devout has more than likely once held
before a flash of light obliterates all beliefs
into the ashes of new beginnings with no need of beliefs.
The brightness, the ceasing of time,
the dying before death can be understood
brings them back to the last of all hope.
I watch the leaves skirt by in the wind.
The cemetery devoid of family mausoleums
and the elaborate upright monuments
where the depictions of the holy stand guard looking down,
contain only ground stones.
Their granite sheen disturbing the chaos of the season
dismiss me from the perfection only death can offer.

I breathe autumn in and release him.
Moving on I think about all the hollowed-out eyes
wandering about with skin itching to be heard,
their teeth chattering in the wind,
their wizened faces twisted in thought
and their heads bowed with nowhere to go.

The Smallness of Being

The stars map out the heavens.
The full moon reaches down.
The sea roars in her solitude.
My face slips into oblivion,
disappearing into darkness,
as my thoughts follow and fly away,
streaming across an ocean who has no need for man.
My thoughts will not meet the dawn.
They will plunge into the indifferent waters
succumbing to the current of her veins,
resting forever in the cold silence of her darkness.
By the next light I will rise and walk along her golden shore.
Behind me her tide will efface each print of bowed
and ambulatory abstraction.
When the zephyr wind blows
caressing the hairs of what's left of my skin,
and the sun hangs over the wind's horizon,
his strokes lengthening in kind and torpid restraint,
I will strip and bathe naked in her cathartic virtue
basking in the holy salt of her womb.
Later, in the gloaming, as the shadows settle in,
I will face a new darkness
and each new thought framed by the light of day
will fly away and vanish once again
into the indifferent waters who have no need for me.

The Young Woman on the Corner

The holiday's aftertaste was long gone.
The commercial fantasies and Hallmark romances were packed away,
and I'm sure the intellectuals
who conjure-up these advertising dreams and maudlin movies
were already hard at work for the next holiday season.
This day's face was pale, cold and distant.
She was on the corner, a thin gray hoody
and whatever garments underneath
her only defense against the breath of a winter
who had bided his time,
but refused to wait any longer.
All week my check engine light occupied every transient thought,
yet I was still was warm.
When I passed her she looked at me,
then realizing the unspoken ways of the streets,
she quickly looked away embarrassed.
She was pretty. Her face was youthful, not far from the dreams
she once must have held so dear to her heart;
for youthfulness should always be a circulating pool of dreams.
Or, for her, maybe it was a pond fed yearly
by surrounding mountains,
with the lily pads veining-out in communal understanding.
Maybe her eyes danced between the hardy green leaves
hoping to catch the frogs playing hide and seek.
Her attention side-tracked by a family of ducks paddling toward her
hoping for a piece of bread from her tiny hand.
Then maybe she looked-up and noticed to her gaiety
a doe and fawn lapping gently from the water's edge.
Her small movements not nearly enough to startle them.
Now she waits for the money to come, her eyes weary,
her body used as she dreams of the needle to fill the void.

Letter to an Unknown Face

Early summer during another sleepless night,
one of many in a lonely stream of sleepless nights,
I was watching the "American Heroes Channel,"
the name recently changed from the "Military Channel."
Sitting there, I found myself wondering about the name change.
I am not saying soldiers are far from heroes, most certainly are,
but every war and every country has its wartime crimes.
Although I must admit I know neither anything of war
nor the force of its horrors on the human psyche or the human heart.
Therefore, who am I to judge how death in its most
visceral nature can distort the soul.
Nor am I a television executive who understands the power of ratings
and the drive to create more for the better, or worse.
On this particular night I was watching
a documentary set in a newly colorized series
titled "Apocalypse WWI."
The narrator commented on the war production of helmets
by French women, similar to what many other women would do
on both sides of the Atlantic during the next world war,
some of the armaments and equipment different, some the same,
but the communitive effort still equal in heroics.
History shows a French woman inserting a letter into a helmet
meant for a soldier with an unknown face and unknown name.
His feet firmly entrenched in the labyrinthian scars of invention.
His eyes set before the fields of barbwire and the scorched earth.
The man, sharing his home with rats and his body with lice,
and his lungs with an unforgiving air conjured-up
by some of history's best minds,
must have felt helpless
against the brutalities of modernity and patriotism.
Again, I found myself wondering what poem,
novel, script, play, or love letters written between two people
held under lock and key for years,
and then found by distant and unknown relatives,
could ever equal the unknown words
wedged in between the inner liner of the helmet
that would not save the hero who would soon understand
what it means to die.

While You Sleep

Once again, we lay side by side,
the bridges of our bodies uncrossed.
Your breathing is steady
and with your back to me
I watch the moon slip through our window pane.
Her long slender fingers reach over me
climbing freely over the terrain of your body.
You sigh contentedly and sleep on.
I turn my sleepless orbit to the clock.
The red-light beams 3:00 AM.
The delimiter's blinking sucks me into nothingness.
I see no beginning, no end, just empty space
of what we never became and what we'll never be.
When you awaken the sun will welcome you
and you will accept his warmth and his promise,
and I'll know neither anything of the moon nor the sun nor you.

The Solitary Bluff

The tide is high
and somber under a gray sky.
Its rhythmic to and fro
gently lap the dunes I sit atop
lost and alone in silent refuge.
The tide's motion reminds me of a woman's hand,
soft in its intent,
caressing the inner thigh of a man,
drowning him with a desire
he has always turned away from.
Lulled into a trance,
I scan the seascape
and watch the impetuous surfers
dip beneath the rolling waves
only to resurface safely on the other side.
They repeat the motion without fear
until they find their spot
and wait for their wave to come in.

Forever Dead

From the eternal elixir
of innocence,
I played and prayed
as a child.
I only knew the love,
the laughter,
and the life of a child.
Then his hand crawled
through the darkness
ransacking the temple
of my first life's body;
stealing the eternal
heart of happiness and hope;
leaving me with nothing
but the memory of despair
and an empty shell
of corrupted flesh
held together and
propped up by the
poles of lonely
and savage bones.
The child in me
forever dead.

Butterflies on Windshields

The mountains, clothed in their final vicissitudes
of blazing yellows, reds and oranges,
arose on either side of our car like sentinels at an unknown gate.
I watched her through the distance of the rearview mirror.
She was perched high in her seat like a princess.
I smiled as she climbed the scars of time's icy advance
and the upheaval of its temperate retreat.
Beneath the canopies' death throes
some of the mountains' faces were sheared smooth,
other parts jagged, some contained the texture of both,
but no two areas were alike,
and not one was more profound than the next.
A life lesson I thought.
And how proud and enamored I was with that thought.
In the future, I imagined myself explaining to her
the analogy between the mountains and the many faces of life;
how each face holds a history in the scars and lines left behind,
a history that may unveil a little about ourselves
if we look closely enough.
Then she would find me mild and wise, her papa.
Holding onto this image my eyes moved down
to the tender and wild blooms hugging the roadside.
I spotted Bull Thistles, Devil's Paintbrushes, Asiatic Day Flowers,
and, interspersed like a universe of setting suns,
the common Dandelion.
Their colors were arrayed like an impressionist's painting.
It was the season's last splash of life.
I gripped the wheel and leaned forward
thinking what analogy of mine could grow
from this earthly glory of time and perennial wisdom.
Then, out of nowhere,
arising from the canvas of my borrowed thought,
a speck of black and orange ebullience
fluttered into the path of my windshield.
As the creature nose-dived into the loneliness of the concrete,
a metamorphosis of another kind,
I looked into the rearview mirror
only to see her staring straight ahead,
with tears welling in her eyes.
My heart dropped.
The image of myself was gone left by the roadside.
What in this world can I tell her she will not learn for herself?

Behind the Veneer is Vulnerability

She leaned forward, her phone in her hands.
She propped her forearms on the bar for leverage.
From over her shoulder, I watched a video of her at the firing range.

The figures milling about in the video,
all males draped in commonplace masculinity,
seemed like inconsequential shades let loose
on an earthy canvas where she was the locus of power,
with one meaty hand thrust-out behind her to counter the kickback.

Her hair spilled down from beneath her hat.
Her eyes followed the barrel to an unknown target beyond.
Her face was shielded like Goya's depiction
of murderers lost in the sudden darkness of May.
Her breasts shaping her sweater,
as the slow-motion action of the video
underscored the dramatic scene of a woman
staking her claim in a so-called man's world.

If I allowed my mind its usual trajectory,
dipping into the psychoanalytical world
begun by Freud and continued by his better, Lacan;
I would have centered on the gun as phallus, not the lack of it,
but her subconscious desire for it, replacing the father.

That would have been unfair, weak and unkind.
Yet was it better for me to follow the undeniable
curves of her hard body with a hard eye,
attempting to gain a spot in this world of hyper-masculinity,
forgoing my romantic self to look down the barrel of my own lust?

I remember an image of her sitting before a fireplace,
her left arm bearing the weight of her body,
her legs pressed together and angled slightly at her knees,
her feet set apart like partially open scissors,
her body warming as the breath of the fire suffused the valley
of her spine.

She was pensive and remote.
The world around her drunk with delight.
When she spoke, she spoke softly.
When she wasn't speaking her head was bowed.
If she felt my eyes, I hope they were weightless and kind
as they peered into her tableau of vulnerability.

Twilight

When I first moved onto my street
there was a good number of children
and they all played together in multicultural happiness.

I remember one evening pulling into my driveway,
the kids scattered in my front yard
playing a game I didn't pick-up on.
Even if I did realize what they were playing,
I'm sure I wouldn't have remembered the logistics anyway.

Adulthood possesses a swift and silent proclivity for thievery.

As I looked at them, they all stopped
wide-eyed and unmoving,
like ancient statues standing upright
amid the fallen ruins that once housed them.
The sky above their heads their only ceiling.

The little girl from the family across the street,
the only child not locked in a sudden fear,
sat on a ball and casually looked at me,
her brown eyes free from cloudiness.
Her gaze bespoke quick intelligence.
She turned back to the statues surrounding her,
and told them not to worry, I was okay.

She could have been Scout and I a hero less, Boo.
Stepping over my threshold, a surge of remembrance reshaped me
hearing the commotion and the laughter of life filling my house
with the fructified present and a past that had long been misplaced.

Then things happened. Families broke-up.
Some of the kids disappeared with the schisms,
others grew-up, and the streets beyond the
protective eyes of their parents echoed
with voices no longer children's.

I didn't notice anything but the quiet.
My street was like a snow toppled street.
Silent even at the apex of several intervening summers
growing more aggressive and un-mirthful of the freshet lives
playing in the holiness of youth everywhere.

Still, a childless street didn't touch me with regret
until the next generation moved in.
Now their laughter has blessed my street
once again with character and charm.
A laughter unbound by the news,
the violence confining the air,
the increasing chasm between the rich and the poor,
the poisoned ethos of racial superiority,
and the duplicity of social media eroding away our democracy.

The windows beyond my television screen hold the future in a dusk
still kind as the kinetic force behind it withdraws its growing fury.

And I hope their laughter will never alter in spirit
no matter what the future portends.

The Other Side of the Wall

The river below us moved serenely
beneath the ancient light of the heavens.
Conscious of the night sounds and the mythic spell of firelight
the river tempered his voice in deference to her.

Above the reach of the fire's fingertips,
those perennial torches of humankind,
I could see her face beyond the flames
meandering through the ruins of faraway thought.

I lifted my eyes and followed the dying embers
burning-up in flight;
each one disappearing unceremoniously
into the starry specter of space and time.
When she began to intone softly,
as if the darkness demanded it, of her inability to smile,
my gaze, bordering on the psychedelic,
was bouncing from one constellation to the next.

As she continued to speak, I looked at her
and felt she had always known
I had a tendency to judge her.
Whether she knew I'd always found her eyes keen,
her mind astute, and her heart strong and brave, I don't know.
Still, my assessment of her was always there,
at times fair and flattering, and other times—not.

Beneath the stars my judgment was at the ready,
and I listened intently as she dropped her guard
and explained how one day after work
she practiced smiling in the rearview mirror of her car,
and nothing she did could get the mirror to smile back.

Missing the severity and sincerity of her confessional,
the faces gathered around the eternal promise
of firelight found other reasons
to make her the primary prop for the night's jokes—
someone had to be.

Later, in bed and coming down from the stars,
I wondered how the young woman on the other side of the wall,
pretty and desirable, and who has traveled to distant cities
and foreign lands, was unable to discover her smile.

By the morning she was gone, and a strange
and savage loneliness stood judge over me.
Later in the day her mother drove me down a gravel road
to a neighboring pond,
and as we waded in the water we talked deeply and devoutly,
something we always did, the two of us.

When she told me that in the morning
her daughter curled-up in bed next to her
and wondered why everyone was making fun of her,
my heart ached for the daughter who has always intrigued me.
Then I realized, quite plainly, I had failed to understand the voice
the daughter herself was desperately trying to understand.

With the sun shining down kindly
and the autumn sprinkled sparsely in the trees,
a deep regret over my insensitivity seized me,
and my mind fumbled for the cadence of her voice,
which passed me by so easily in the amusement of the night.
As her mother and I traveled back up the gravel road,
in between the gaps of a new conversation,
I felt if I were a man, compassionate and strong,
I would lose my smile in honor of the unknown woman on
the other side of the wall.

Eyes Unseen

The inherent meaning of her name is "Victory of the People."
The spiritual connotation means "Overcomer."
When she first approached me,
I was doing my best to conceal myself
behind the column rising from the elbow of the bar.
I remember the night well: it was a cold February night.
Outside, the moon was effaced by an endless stream of clouds
and the sky was empty; devoid of the stars,
and the faraway places a dreamer needs to slip away to
when the tangible reality that encumbers his world
becomes too vitriolic and barren
of the slightest notion of human kindness.
Neil Young's "Cortez the Killer" had just begun to play.
My knitted winter hat was beginning to slide down my forehead
half covering my eyes, which were slipping into to space,
pondering the might and sin of imperialism,
and the soon-to-be-suffering Aztec people.
A culture where, according to Neil Young,
and before Cortez's fleet slithered across the tranquility of their shore,
"Hate was just a legend and war was never known."
I looked up from my beer
and noticed her walking over with a pool cue in hand.
She leaned in and complimented me on my choice of song and hat.
I nodded my head, smiled and thanked her.
She said "you're welcome," returned the smile and walked away.
Every now and again I would look up from my beer
and steal a glance at her.
Her lithe body moved effortlessly around the pool table.
I was taken in by the subtle nuances of her movements,
and the seemingly controlled awareness of her own sensuality.
After I finished my beer I went to the bathroom.
Washing my hands, I wondered whether or not
the moon was now free to show her face
over a city stuck in the doldrums of the mid-winter blues.
Drying my hands, I looked into the mirror, tilted my head,
and saw nothing but the dead eyes
of ineffectuality staring back at me.
When I opened the bathroom door,
she was sitting in the chair next to mine.
She was showing the bartender, her friend,
something on her phone.
As her friend handed her phone back to her
something familiar on the screen flashed by my eyes.
I heard her friend say that was good

52

before walking away to the other end of the bar,
and she moved back over to the pool table.
As I watched her begin her dance around the table again,
the cue sliding back and forth through her fingers with ease,
I had this gut feeling that they had just read an obscure poem of mine;
a poem where the speaker had been left unguarded.
Then the mixed feelings of being flattered and exposed
arose in me like an opiate induced dream.
A dream where the surrealism flowers into a vast hopefulness
and then suddenly withers away into a hopeless nightmare.
After that first night, whenever we were in the bar together,
she would try to get me to open up, but where I felt unguarded,
I quickly re-erected the walls—
walls I would not allow her to breach,
and I walked away every night with bowed head,
feeling the roots of my ineffectuality growing deeper and stronger
like an unfortunate truth strangling every ounce of my being.
When she wasn't there a strange loneliness suffused within me,
and then I figured I must be alive somewhere, somehow.
After a little while she finally gave up on me—
who could blame her?
Then we were reduced to quick glances of emptiness.
Then months went by without me seeing her
and on a lonely Friday night, belonging to another winter,
I looked up from my beer and found her surrounded by friends
sitting near the column where we first spoke to each other.
That night every time I looked at her I felt like Rimbaud,
who pulled "Beauty down" on his knees and "cursed her."
I cannot say I found "her embittered."
It was I who shunned her kindness
averting my eyes from her thoughtful gaze.
I left the bar around 1:30 in the morning.
At home, alone, it was 8:30 before sleep overtook me.
My thoughts were scattered and I chased after every one of them.
When my thoughts circled back to her,
I couldn't shake the feeling that never in my life
did I desire more than to have the name bearer
whole heartedly attached to the attributes her name carries.
Even if her personality isn't shaped within the meanings of her name,
it wouldn't bother me in the least;
that hope is nothing more than a foolish dream
conjured-up by a foolish dreamer who shares very little with anybody.
What I'm really sorry about, when it comes to her,
is that I don't even know the color of her eyes.

Lost Nights

In the gray dawn,
in the silent moments before
the first rays of the sunlight,
the night slowly retreats without complaint,
like a neophyte leaving a candle filled room for the ordained.
The tiny flames flickering from the esoteric breaths
the ordained feel is theirs' to utter.

Beyond my blinds the scene rolls-out,
everything beyond holds to a sleep
that for me refused to come.
The memory of you is too strong.
Your touch, a ghost's lingering touch,
is a nearness that is unmistakable.
The day will be empty, I think.
Your memory aping my every step.

I remember those nights,
the thunder rumpling the darkness,
your eyes flashing with the lightning,
while the syncopation of the rain against the window sill
was drumming with the rhymes of our heart beats,
the embrocation of your voice slipped into my ear
healing the pinning's of my mind.

Mother to Mother

The discordant sounds of the cathedral
of modern medical science reverberated
through the sterile and winding nave of jostling orderlies and nurses.
The clipboards detailing the patients' final fight
aide the medical staff who have chosen to be soldiers
in a war they know they can never win,
no matter how many battles have been won.
It's a sacrifice they themselves must wonder sometimes
why they have chosen this to be their life's mission.
Those who pass them in the halls,
people like me, who are focused-in on one room
and on one patient and on one family,
sometimes fail to see what most of them
must always carry home
and mull over in the silence of their hearts.
I pass room after room thinking
the jargon placed above the sufferers' heads
are the beginning notes of tragically written poems.
Each family sequestered in their misery
wholly embrace the stream of family and friends,
who search and fumble for the right words
they hope will help the family in their healing.
A healing that will now be a continuum of sunrises and sunsets,
with the nightlight of the moon and the stars,
and the spread of the symbolic aurora of eternal Motherhood
saddled in between them, illuminating a new hope.
I reach the last room, my friend's,
his younger brother dutifully standing guard—as only a brother can.
My friend doesn't have much time left on this earth.
A new world is waiting for him, but that doesn't make the hurting
of those who love him any less severe.
The Priest comes in to administer "Last Rites"
and to grant absolution for a man God has chosen to call home.
He is a young Priest, and I am reminded
that the Spirit of the Lord is eternally young.
My friend, a vessel of goodness,
during "The Litany of the Saints,"
draws out the quivering voices
and the tears of everybody touching his body.
When his mother suctions the moisture from his mouth,
her subconscious act as natural as the day he was born,
I am reminded of Mary's misery at the foot of her own Son's agony,
and the moment is now a union of two mother's
whose love and undying grace are virtues
only they can fully understand.

55

Beyond the Frame

She's a friend of the band capturing the chaos and order of the scene.
When she moves my gaze follows, a strange sadness swallows me.
Before her eyes, I feel threadbare, speechless, helpless.
She weaves through the crowd shooting from the best angles.
I don't know her name and maybe never will.
Generally, when a woman's presence carries me along
I'm accustomed to abandoning my gaze once it's discovered,
like a confronted thief drops a tattered bag
internally bejeweled by what is not his.
On this night she moved about the room open but unreadable.
The glint of her tacit allowance
found me over the ranges of unknown heads.
Tethered to her, she drew me across the defile
of my own remoteness of thought.
The moment too honest, I had to look away,
my vulnerability falling on my feet.
The band played on,
the night filling in the crevices of the square beyond.
Staring at my feet, my vulnerability all consuming,
I turned back to her, wondering if she understood.
Her glance tender, direct, reassured me to keep trying.
She slowly started to move back and forth in front of the band.
I looked at her hands, the lightness of her grasp,
the way her body moved.
Her azure eye, beyond time's apathy,
captured what time's willing to forget.
I slid off my barstool facing the band,
searching for her quintessence.
I left the seat open for anybody or nobody
and stood solemnly alone.
She walked over and perched herself on the seat,
and sat with her back to me, her closeness matching her gaze.
I hoped the warmth my body left behind, if there was any,
coalesced with her, forming something warmer,
something intimate,
enkindling an effusion of poetic silence.
I try not to utter the word beauty in any grammatical form,
it has fallen from my limited lexicon dead from abuse.
Prettiness in all its forms has found space on my tongue.
There is humility in pretty's unspoken truth.
The word encapsulating everything the other has lost,
with a smile greater, eyes more serene, a touch more sincere.
Even so, I will not out limn the intimacies of her body's design,

or her long blond hair falling freely over the portrait she creates
until I am able to get lost in the inscape rolling out behind her eyes.
If pressured to describe her and relying on superficialities,
I would answer my inquisitor by saying she reminds me
of a James Bond seductress, intriguing and dangerous,
possessing the uniqueness of being
to coerce a man to the edge of the abyss,
and then at the last second reaching out her hand,
smiling softly, saving the poor bastard from the freefall of mortality.

The Fabric of a Woman

1

I agree with W. H. Auden's maxim that a
writer's cupidity is more dangerous than his or her politics.
Although many writers and poets have stretched out history
by turning their bodies toward the want of another's flesh,
while others have pricked their ears
to the political machines that have
caused the cries of fellow countrymen and women alike.
Their innocence stamped-out
by the cadence of fascism and hate.
The urge in me to map out the borders of the flesh is as precise
as the wish of the most gifted cartographer.
Other times I itch to attack the political machine like a rabid dog.
For whatever reason, the forces that back these urges in me
seem to dissipate as quickly
as a fog withdrawing from an unkempt city
forever somnolent in a mosaic of an uneventful death.

2

Thus, I move on scraping the inner walls of my mind
in the hopes of making something useful out of the everyday,
trying to keep it simple and somehow neutral.
The residue of which produces nothing more of me
than a mere poetaster.
A coward back by a coward's keyboard.
Harsh, I know, but it's a maxim I alone must face.

3

I can't claim to know the history of her ancestry
like Etheridge Knight knew his by the pictures
plastered to his prison cell wall, and the stories remembered by him,
when memory was all he had,
were passed down to him from the familiar voices
rightfully proud and aggrieved in and by generational knowledge.
To be truthful I barely know her at all,
but she became a subject for a pervious poem.
I do know her ancestry came from a divided land

made one by the ravages of war.
For better or for worse, I cannot say,
I have neither the right nor have I suffered
from war and its aftermath. I do know her ancestral land
held in its soil the blood of so many before and after
the fall of a city made tragically iconic
by Walter Cronkite's generational voice.
Her simple gesture made her as subject, right.
Subject is not the right word here—
it's academic, distant, non-generational, safe.

4

There are never words in the bottom of my bottle.
Sometimes there are words the next day
coming to me in fragmented pieces
of a night's worth of fragmented memory.
On this night she was wearing a floral pattern summer dress.
The dominate color of her dress,
in this night's memory anyway, was orange.
Maybe it was red or pink, but like the FBI's mark for Dillinger,
this mistake may have been made
by the lights falling dimly over her,
and I will retain this possible mistake
like history has retained the mistake of Dillinger's final moments.
Rightfully or wrongfully, memory, for all it contains, can be as vivid
as the features contained in the mirror staring back at me.

5

I sat on the image of her in this dress for a while,
waiting for the words, but the words refused to come
and I turned my hopes of salvaging that night
to the faces in the windows rising above the bar,
their eyes keeping watch on the square below.
Then I turned my hopes to the grifters
hanging-out in the shadows by the fountain.
Moving on from them, I turned my thoughts to the woman
nicely framed by the softly lit window of the bar across the
square—still the words refused to come.

6

Then one night like in a dream her image came back to me,
and she reminded me of an actress—
unremarkably pretty and unattainable—
in a movie where the colorization of television was still in its infancy.
I envisioned myself a sailor on shore leave
lost in some unspoken hurt,
and she the distant wish on the other side of the bar.
Her long dark hair was tied up,
the slender and tan nape of her neck visible,
and I remember thinking to myself that the simple act
of tying-up her hair
and the subtle intimacies of her body are poems in themselves.
She moved away from me
after giving me a beer I didn't need to ask for,
and these thoughts came quickly, in between my first couple of sips,
long before reality fades into illusion
and illusion into mental thirst.
When she returned to me,
we talked over a ridge that seemed level,
yet was different somehow.
She moved along on a higher plain with a spirit hopeful,
living in a body contoured by the dress
that would not relinquish its hold over me
that I was nothing more than a drunkard
on the other side waiting for the world to end.
I should have turned back to the intimacies of her body,
the umbrella of her breath, the anodyne of her fingertips,
the strength of her dark eyes, her smile's warmth
and then sudden gloom.
That would have been too easy death had already staked its
claim over me. Dream over.

The Intuition of an Artist

As her bandmate fingered his fretboard,
she turned on her seat and sat in profile.

Her chin rested on her fiddle and mine in my hand.
The crown of her head was dipped toward me.
In a lissome tableau of womanhood,
she drew her bow over the strings.
I could see the shade of her eyeshadow
and the seductive curl of her eye lashes,
and I knew the dramatic story of her body
was gracefully holding every eye in the place.
The timbre of her soul felt in every lonely note.

Sitting there listening to her,
I felt an intimacy in our positioning,
as if the simple juxtaposition of our bodies
collapsed the space between us.

We were acquaintances sometimes seemingly
edging toward something more profound,
but lacking the art of confabulation I'd regress
and our conversations were always brief,
revolving around our admiration and love of music and its creators.
I felt safe on the ecumenical bridge of the rhythm and blues.
The subterranean pulses that comprise us still muted.
The drumming of our heartbeats impersonal.

They were playing, The Beatles', "Let it Be."
When she turned forward and leaned into her mic
singing of Mary's wisdom,
I had to turn away from her. I was flooded with the feeling
that she was singing just for me, perhaps as a go between,
a celestial hand on her shoulder urging her forward,
or maybe just from the mystical will of an artist,
who emotively drew from me what I needed and didn't expect.
My finger slipping under my glasses to wipe away the tears.

At that moment, amid the lyrics and the music,
and the rolling thoughts in between,
we were part of the agape.
Her soulful understanding, her kindness, her prettiness
and her voice, a hope in our little square of humanity.

This was not a moment for thaumatology.
Maybe it was an inner locution
that she herself wasn't quite aware of,
a moment to be dissected in the deep nights deprived of sleep?
Either way, it is pleasing to sink your feet
into the waters of magical realism
contemplating how the metaphysical world
can reach out of the void touching the temporality,
if only temporary, of an artist and a fan.

Left Unguarded

I sat beneath the sway of a dim barroom light,
tucked safely away in the corner, with nothing but dead space
and a door to the unknown world stretching-out behind me.
I watched her working underneath the lights running above the bar.
She was dressed in black,
with every fiber of every thread shaping her design.
From around her neck hung layered shapes the color of wheat.
The same could be seen hanging from her ears, just a little obscured,
concealed behind the dark forest of hair.
She moved in between the rise of alcohol
and a line of furtive eyes glazed over with thirst.
Untouched by the hands of phantom ownership
she settled on the slump-over specter which was me.
In the hush tones bridging the gap between admirer and admired
we talked about the limitless longing of human desire.
With word after word suspended in the clamor of the barroom night,
I told her she was nothing more than "disarming."
And she, with the youthful eyes of a seldom seen truth,
walked away to the opposite end of the bar,
the word wedged between us in silence.
I suppose I could have told her that her eyes
were the glimmer and calm sailors dream by;
or her face the obsession of painters;
or her laughter the melody dancing beyond the darkness;
or her body the supple wish of lonely hands.
My problem would have been to what point and to what end.
Similar things have been said, equally trite, all dead.
After a few moments, moving with the ease that brought the word
to the surface in the first place, she made her way back to me
voicing her displeasure with the word's ambiguity.
Reassured the word wasn't intended to be adversarial,
and it lay in the substance she couldn't see, but always offered,
she frankly said, "I don't care. I don't like it."
In the end, after everything was said, it really didn't matter,
she just walked away with my last defense dangling from her hand,
leaving me alone and unguarded,
and the light above my head no less dim than when the conver-
sation first started.

The Civilized World

The child's cry rattles the night.
The unseen hands of Heaven and Hell
are there before the first tear falls.
The demons snicker with delight.
While the angels bow their heads,
weeping with tears foreign to ours.
A world free, austere and irreverent,
continues on with the impulsion of daily does and wants,
giving its dual impressions of right and wrong,
before moving on secure in a world rightfully civilized.
Forgetting about the flight of the Holy Family,
the blue latex hands of Civil Authority,
dirty and unsympathetic,
thump the Bible with one hand
and scrounge the worn
and honest pockets of the refugees with the other.
Unfeeling fingers, far from this boarder of despair,
seize the trinkets of a former life
and the small articles of faith
emblematic of the refugees' hope and flight.
With an angel's pristine truth,
the child's hand cleaves the night.
Dissevered from her mother's hand,
she reaches up to claim an object of faith
blurred by the breeched levees of her brown eyes.
Her hand is brushed away,
it drops like a dead butterfly in the uneasy night.
A rosary tossed away and trampled into the dust of despair
oozes with the fresh blood of innocence.

Oneness

I stepped through the church doors,
reached for the stoup
and withdrew my hand,
forgetting about the sand.
"Like a grain and nothing more,
ubiquitous and commonplace," I thought.
I crossed the vestibule feeling invisible.
Entering the main body of the church
I went to the table and reached for a palm.
Only the scrapes from the previous mass.
At the rough edge of the
memory of a quick glance,
I think there may have
been three left behind.
Unwilling to allow myself
to say perfectly, "Three,"
I'll chalk-up the moment to
the fleeting hope of symbolic import.
I reached for the largest one
not waiting for the usher
to replenish the tabletop.
Stepping into the foot of the nave,
I genuflected at my spot
and slid into the pew.
I slipped off of the pew,
bowed my head and closed my eyes.
Settling back into the pew,
I reached for my palm
and ran my hand along it
like an ancient mercenary his blade.
It was withered—still decaying.
Behind me, I heard the usher
scattering fresh palms over the table.
I remained seated content with what found me.

Supplication in Our Sickness

Early spring, the tatters of winter's long blanket
has seeped into the softening fecundity stirring below.
The breath of the former season has grown less bitter,
even though in his stubbornness
he'll still breathe over the land,
reminding us he's fighting until the end.
No longer encumbered, the brown fields
roll-out like an undulating and turbid sea.
Soon another season will bring to the surface
the plush green life emblematic
of a summer still able cultivate his gifts for us
beneath his own reach of growing fury.
Children will run inside the mazes
that have reshaped nations.
They will run through the day,
their laughter lifting, following close behind.
Then the sunburnt haze will
coalesce with the slow spread of twilight,
as Levine's first star of night surfaces.
Dreams nurtured in the mazes
waft-up encapsulated within
the withdrawing beams of last light.
The beacons dotting the landscape
begin to set ablaze the country side
waiting for the dreamers' safe return.
The men and women who till the land
will scrape the dirt from beneath their fingernails,
relieved that their labor was spent in earnest.
Their salt and growing sorrow is a sacrifice
only their kin can fully understand.
Later, young lovers will find themselves beside the growing fields.
The shadows accepting the earthy pleasure of their song.
The following silence over an age lost settles in with the darkness,
never to return to the dreams
that transform into the things of foolishness.
Lonely old men and women will fall asleep beside open windows.
Their welcoming bodies caressed by the night breeze
will awaken early, the new day dawning.
They will look out over the sea of green
and watch the morning breeze rippling along the surface,
hoping their prayers will be answered,
and life will break through the news of a near future closing in on us.

Lady Picasso

1

Sometimes, in the slanting strokes of the withdrawing sun,
our words float between us like dust motes looking for a spot to land.
Other times our words strike like lightning,
storing-up energy in the silence of unexpected thought.

On one particular evening she handed me her phone.
Her guard down, her power at the ready,
she let loose part of her oeuvre.
From over my shoulder,
she pointed out the beatitudes of her vision,
doing her best to show me the nuances of her work.

Her phone failed her profoundly,
withholding the marrow of each piece.
She left me alone, her words falling helplessly from her lips.
I leaned forward trying to explore her work on my own.
I could feel her—I wanted to speak but my fear swallowed me.

Most compliments, if not all, are nothing but solitary cages,
refusing any pardons and devoid of any escapes.
Thus, I stared introspectively into space holding onto my silence.
In the waiting, her phone turned into a dark empty canvas.

I opened her phone scrolling through her work again.
Vision after vision plunged me deeper into silence.
Stopping on a piece of her brother and his child,
I slipped into a trance, turning inward, dreaming of her.

2

She crossed the cobblestone square,
her steps holding the morning quiet
as she walked toward the Bateau-Lavoir.
Her thoughts, her work, was evolving with the new century,
only four-years-old now, with the promise of a new vision,
and a new voice breathing heartache
into the universal consciousness.
The air was still in the murky blue dawn.
The last vestige of sleep heavy in the transition.
She was new to the area.
She was selling her work on the corners

when he first caught sight of her.
Ever since their first meeting he had taken her in under his tutelage.
Around the salons, amid the voices of other
poets and artists, she was affectionately,
and with some jealousy, known as Lady Picasso.

3

She stood before the old building.
She listened for the creaking voice of the restless timbers.
The building remained silent in the morning calm.
She looked to the east. Her sadness pretty, untouchable—
a solemn portrait of womanhood.
Her eyes watched the horizon shaping the first faint red of morning.

4

His easel stood in the corner.
The shutters beyond closed.
His canvas lifeless in the waiting.
She opened a jar of his red paints,
reached for one of his brushes,
dipped it in and stirred it up before
writing "Rosy-Fingered Dawn"
across the top of his canvas.
She set the brush down
and walked over to her easel.
She opened the battered shutters.
The reach of the morning, finding the smallest openings,
seeped into the darkest corridors.
She looked at the mouth of an alleyway,
the captive feet held by vagrant misery and spent pleasure,
still entwined by the nameless limbs of night,
became restless beneath the earth's withdrawing blanket.
The ramparts of the alley's brick facades
entombed the cries of their prisoners,
cries of pleasure and pain and loss and un-gain.
She looked away, her understanding too sharp,
too keen to the stories left behind in alleyways.
She closed her eyes and tilted her head toward the square.
She could envision the canopy of trees coming to life.
The birds' ritual filling the air in a rendition of newness.
She sat before her canvas and reached for her chalk.
She started to sketch an emotive image she kept in the silence
of her heart.
Her eyes shining with a vulnerability she could not conceal.

5

He slipped in quietly with his Montauk shorts twisted from sleep.
With the dawn fully accomplished
and the heat of the new day spreading,
he knew the day would be long and hot.
Where was his muse, he thought?
He removed his nautical striped shirt,
revealing his bronze Mediterranean chest.
Her own sweater had long been removed,
revealing the nape of her neck, the narrow spread of her shoulders,
and the nakedness of her capable arms.
She undid her long brown hair, letting fall naturally over her back.
They looked at each other. Their eyes saying all.
Her unblemished dark eyeliner from the night before
reminded him of modernity's Cleopatra.
She faced her canvas and returned to her work.
He sat before his canvas, his mind turning.
As he read what she scrolled, a smile was beginning to spread,
his face lifting from the blue claiming his thought, his hand.
He looked at the hard of his brush, and twisted his body,
stretched out his legs and crossed his feet.
He yearned for change, a new color of inspiration
stirring within some physical or metaphysical force—or both.
He studied the canvas of her arm.
It was a face he did not recognize.
He would years later as an artist of a different form,
whose emotive powers would die before his own.
The face familiar to the nighthawks in lonely diners
and the boulevards shaped by broken dreams.

6

He looked-up at her canvas coming to life.
He followed the Spartan image of her brother.
His eyes tracing the lines of her brother's protruding jaw,
his chiseled chest, his broad shoulders and his sinewy arms.
He was holding his child against his chest heart to heart.
Their drumming the same, yet different.
He lifted from his accoutrements a fresh brush,
dipped it into the same red paint stirring it up again.
He paused and looked at her.
He closed his eyes.
He softly inhaled and then exhaled.
He wasn't quite sure what he was trying to breathe-in then release.

He opened his eyes. She was lost in her own work.
He faced his canvas writing—mother, breast, child, rose.
Then he wrote "Lady Picasso" proud of his discovery.
He looked at her. Her stroke poetic in perfect aloneness.
He faced his canvas again.
He crossed out Lady Picasso
and set his brush down dreaming of a rose.

Aside a River

At this moment it's dusk, your arms are folded over your breasts,
your head is bowed, your unseen eyes are
following the landscape of your mind.
The weakening glow of the sun
suffusing its last light across a pink horizon
falls in silent reverence around you.
The river kindly carving out the river bank
drowns out the crunch beneath each footstep.
I can only guess that your thoughts are steady
as the river's murmur eases you into contemplation.
I close my book—a book on Jesus of Nazareth,
setting it on the armrest of my chair and watch you.
You pass under the river birches branching out,
their diamond shape leaves dance above your head,
yet you seem not to notice. You are a poet's delight.
A gray streak of a mockingbird swoops in
landing on the branches above your head.
Enthralled, he is watching you understanding his silence is needed.
As he flies from branch to branch keeping pace,
I realize his desire for you is as strong as mine is,
only his will is stronger, and I can imagine his eyes
blinking away with the shutter and admiration of a camera lens
framing the last of the sun caressing your dark hair.
I close my eyes for a second turning inward—nothing.
I rejoin the scene, pick up my book and move to the door.
I fumble with the door knob and watch you,
words escape me, my smile starts only to fade into nothingness,
nebulized inside me where no songs are heard.
With the mockingbird still dutifully at his post,
I move inside and sit at the computer and open my book.
I look at my notes and begin a poem about sin and death—my own.
I pause and gather my life looking out the window.
The river is unchanged moving serenely
beneath the deepening darkness,
and you are out of sight alone with your thoughts
moving somewhere beyond the borders of my mind.
I lean back in my chair and can hear his trilling,
his simple serenade, not his own, drifting back to me.
I can envision him above your head, the night soft without design,
and I pray "The Beast Within" will relent just for one night.

71

The Beast Within

The beast from within I have known.
I have indulged his evil ways.
I felt his claws and heard his groan
and knew Satan's laughter and praise.

From the ominous darkness deep,
the restless beast moved from under,
destroying my innocent sleep
and ripping my soul asunder.

The animal and I conformed
in the sudden blaze of desire,
and in the stench the minions swarmed
released from hell's eternal fire.

In the horrible dread of night,
succumbing to his evil urge,
my hands felt the strength of his might
and my pulsating blood his surge.

Unable to escape this bane,
the beast continued to devour,
as I turned ugly and profane
consumed by his beastly power.

And now among the dead I dwell
in unending nocturnal strife,
while the dove's diurnal death knell
connotes my daily loss of life.

Final Supplication

Lord, help me to unclench
his fist that grips my heart;
relieve me from this evil wrench
that's bent on tearing me apart;

steer me through life's maddening toil,
calm the ragging tempest of my soul,
assuage the winds' buffeting turmoil
that's keeping me from my life's simple role;

pluck me from the soil of the dead,
grant me the vision to see the flowers,
which slowly blossom and softly spread,
swaying in the wisdom of quiet hours;

but Lord, if his hand still wants its fill,
and in strength the winds gain,
and blindness dominates the flowers' will,
end this life, end this pain.

From a Darkened Door

From a darkened door,
she waved me in,
a barely dressed whore,
an invitation to sin.
Where is the blame,
is it with me or with her?
I don't feel any shame,
so, I guess, I'm really not sure.
I would enter again,
her lair of lust,
to bed with my friend
and call it a must.
Some people would say
this lascivious need
is a lonely decay
from which the lonely feed.
I would not deny
them their self-righteous acumen.
I simply would reply
we are only human.
On this empty night,
she offered me something more.
She held me tight
like I never felt before.
I cried on her breasts
as she stroked my hair
allowing me rest
from my hidden despair.
Then with one unpaid,
soft and simple kiss,
she out of the night made
a moment of unexpected bliss.
So, in the end,
the only sin I can see,
is me calling my friend
that unkind word's harsh identity.

The Guitar Player

From across a dark and smoky bar
I saw music form into pain
as he strummed his lonesome guitar
and his notes fell like tears of rain.

Refusing the crowd his face,
with his wide gaze scanning the floor,
his foot kept the pace
of his eyes slowly rising shore.

He felt the abyss of his song and rhythm.
Being dispossessed of any defense
he continued to play them
at his own fatal expense.

At every falling note
and every hopeless word
his desperation was growing less remote
as his end was tragically heard.

The lyrics were all forewarning.
Thus, it came as no surprise
when by the following morning
he was dead before sunrise.

A Life Never Lived

From the kindling of my own lie
spreads the flame of selfish desire.
I will stretch out my arms to die
in this all-consuming fire.

Do not, over my death, lament.
I only took never to give.
I never discovered what love meant
or how to passionately live.

Do not adorn my gravestone
with the splendor of living flowers.
Let me lie barren and alone
bereft of life's fertile powers.

On the stone display no trace
as the cold wind blows
over the buried disgrace
of the life never lived lying below.

My Last Night on Earth

Through the remorseful tears
of my brutal crime,
the truth has penetrated
my years of confined time.

I have thought about him
and his sudden life,
and his undone years
that fell from my extended knife.

Some day after tomorrow
I hope to meet him soon,
if God will allow this gift after
my death beneath the morning moon.

My repentance has been long
and arduous I'll explain,
and I will thank him for forgiving me
for all the senseless pain.

There will be no chance
for a last-minute reprieve.
In my death, I hope his family,
if they're able, will be somewhat relieved.

For now, my last night
on this revolving earth,
I dream of you lying
beside our love's lasting worth.

Outside this barred world,
beyond this blighted window pane,
your image takes form
through the streaks of rain.

Our daughter is at rest enclosed
in your faithful hold,
protected from this raging tempest
and the merciless cold.

You are lost and sleepless,
engulfed in all your fears
trying to guess at the
trajectory of unknown years.

I wish I could ease your pain
in this my last dream,
and kiss your image through
the roving searchlights clock-like stream.

I know I have abandoned you
in your frailty and youth,
leaving you alone to raise
the symbol of our love's truth.

Please, one last time, just kiss her for me,
and let her know that my wasted time
hurt everybody I trust and care for,
and that she is our only perfect rhyme.

I hope you fall in love again.
You should never be alone,
and I hope his love is humble and true,
and he loves our daughter as he would his own.

I know the ways of redemption
in this world are controlled by man,
and I shall never be redeemed
by his corporeal hand.

Still, in your love,
forgiveness I will ask,
as I am dissolved of hatred
and have removed my final mask.

I pray that you can
find the ability to forgive,
and understand I always loved you,
although I never discovered how to give.

Believe me that in my love
I have always been true,
and have felt the holiness
of your love's lasting virtue.

I know in my final walk
you won't be there.
Please find my grave
and tend it with care.

78

I will whisper your name
with my dying breath,
and I hope to love you
beyond this world of death.

I have prayed to God
in His right to gift redemption,
trusting He will lift me
from my road of perdition.

If this be ordained
by the Eternal Three,
I will meet you again
by the calm of eternity's sea.

An Age Gone

Sweet silent summer of spent youth.
  Yesteryear's golden age.
    Fades into memory's lost truth,
     and diminishing stage.

An age long before reality
  uncoiled to strike and steal
    the false mask of eternity
      and the youth's pure ideal.

And now, long after all the lies,
  and reality's theft,
    I must stare through corrupted eyes
     at the vacancy left.

Eternal Child

I heard a voice from within the realms of sleep,
saying from my mind's caverns deep,
"Behold the eternal child
forever meek, forever mild."

"Behold the little boy's smile,
sit and listen to his laughter awhile.
Believe that behind his young eyes
is where the simple truth lies."

"Behold the little girl at rest,
softly sleeping on her mother's breasts.
Note her gentle countenance, her gentle breath,
are the enemies of death."

Then the voice said, "In every child you will find
the ways of true life you left behind.
Don the mantle of the child's truth,
and take pleasure in the ways of eternal youth."

From the Rising Laughter of Children

As the pink-rimmed close of night
overcomes the fading of the light,
the children run and play
silhouetted against the pleasant close of day.

Their voices' echo through the sky
recalling remembrances of years gone by,
and amid the children's collective voice,
I rediscover the means to rejoice.

From the vagaries of yesteryear
springs forth a silent tear.
Looking toward the ascending moon
I am raised by childhood gentlest boon.

My childhood has long since diminished,
an age this world brutally finished.
Now as their laughter subsides,
in my heart, a piece of childhood still resides.

A Hope

Atop the spacious hills of golden hue,
in the deep regions of star speckled night,
I sought your holiness lovely and true,
amid the natural beams of sacred light;
but I failing beneath Your holy eye
saw a dense darkness spreading far and wide,
crawling across a once luminous sky,
obscuring Your brilliance on every side.
Your light once known, but my defiant acts,
the chronicler of impetuous days,
darkened Your words of penitential tracts,
permitting evil his serpentine ways.
       May I, through your own celestial powers,
       find the radiant words of contrite hours

Until We Meet Again

There she was always giving me her best,
granting me shelter from the call of death.
She was my needful and singular rest
from life's unforgiving and rancid breath;
but now she is gone, this world she has left
and in the trees the birds no longer sing.
They too feel the silence of her life's theft
and know the torment her absence does bring.
I failed her where she had never failed me,
and on my tongue I taste life's useless myrrh,
grieving her sweet love's sudden vacancy,
lost and alone in a world without her.
      And I'll wait till death forever forlorn
      hoping to see her and to be reborn.

The Beacon

Was I cast out from all humanity,
set adrift atop a turbulent sea,
besieged by its waves' dark insanity,
or was I lost in the darkness of me?
Roving thunder clapped-out its loud command,
as lightning split a malevolent sky.
This violent tempest I could not remand
with the dark madness I could not defy.
Then I descried amid the slant of rain,
in between the rolling fall and ascent,
within a harbor's welcoming domain,
a beacon of safe and tranquil intent.
      And I hope within this light I will find
      a stillness to alleviate my mind.

Duplicity

What permanence could I ever give you,
with a heart fair, unfair, always fickle;
when I first embrace life's sacred virtue,
then spread for death's dissevering sickle?
When I smile and life is beyond compare,
I view humanity's sphere with delight,
but with a swift change comes complete despair,
then I mired in the turbid flows of night.
If I could offer you a steady hand,
with open palm, where beats an honest heart,
I would, but enslaved by my soul's command
I'm lost in duplicity's changing art.
　　　　But what better art is there than your love
　　　　that trumps duplicity's dark reign above?

The Unclean Heart

Her sacredness atop the midnight dew
was unveiled in the walled flower garden,
just as the nightingale quietly flew
and my lonely heart began to harden.
Her truth illuminated by the light
of the moon. Her naked body was lent
but my lone heart being less than forthright
rejected her body's willing consent.
Underfoot the flowers began to close
as I turned from her to forever leave.
Refusing the love of an open rose
I knew I forewent love's final reprieve.
       The unclean heart, cold, desolate and dry,
       will always find reasons to let love die.

The Sentimentality of Youth

Through the sun's slanting strokes you first appeared
enwrapped in the golden caress of youth,
and I espied what I terribly feared
of your sublime body's burgeoning truth.
Watching you across an anguished distance
you could not feel the sad track of my gaze
that followed your body's new existence
through the setting sun's early evening haze.
We were both young, but I older than you,
stood speechless as you slowly walked away,
and you moving gradually out of view
could not see my head lowered in dismay.
      You will never know the sadness you bring
      to a lonely heart terrified to sing.

The Untouchable

With a sublime and tragic intensity,
she spoke of flowers from a foreign land
possessing a gentle propensity
toward death when touched by a human hand.
The flowers, she explained, would simply die
at the slightest or the most corrupt clutch.
Transfixed by her passion, I wondered why
she loved what could not withstand human touch.
Was there something wicked out of her past?
Did some unthinkable and savage hand
strip away her innocence way too fast,
stealing it by his hard and vile command?
      But I decided I would not infer
      on flowers that are unequal to her.

Sterile

Her soft green eyes would hold me suspended.
At sight her smile made my heart beat distraught.
When she laughed my soul was apprehended,
but she was much too young I wrongly thought.
Thus, I searched for a more refined flower,
trying to usurp her from my arid mind,
but I rooted within her soil's power
was too weak leaving her garden behind.
From a parched distance I take her in:
a woman spreading forth in subtle grace.
Now I must look away with hurt chagrin,
as I wither in some dark-barren place.
      From the things I was terrified to know
      my heart stagnates and refuses to grow.

Lust in Action

What undesirable force has led me
into this hopeless land barren and dark?
Was it some beast I was too blind to see?
Did he on my heart leave his evil mark?
Yes, but I chose him through a feral lust
to eclipse with pleasure women's treasure.
In this darkness I'm chained with the unjust;
a sentence dealt out in proper measure.
Now I must look away when women pass.
My savage heart is broken and unclean.
My countenance is hideous and crass.
My ravenous gaze is starving and mean.
   And now I know this terrible disgrace
   is a punishment I cannot erase.

Upon Viewing the Ecstasy of St. Teresa

Standing beneath her holy ecstasy,
enrapt in the folds of her marble's white,
was the angel's flaming spear fantasy
or was the flame Heaven's pulsating light?
In the angel's hand rose the golden spear
in preparation for a mighty thrust,
while at the tip shimmered the fiery fear
of all she desired, loved and prayed to trust.
After the spear penetrated her heart
her body shivered with celestial pain.
The spear seemed bent on tearing her apart
as it brought her beneath God's holy reign.
      And now her ecstasy is wholly clear
      staring through the blur of every last tear.

Shawn McCann lives in Syracuse, New York. He works for the City of Syracuse as a Plans Examiner II in the office of the Fire Prevention Bureau. He has earned a Master of Arts Degree from SUNY Empire State College. This is his debut collection of poetry.